Metamorphosis

Kaylah McDonald

BookLeaf Publishing

Presentation by *BookLeaf Publishing*

Web: www.bookleafpub.com

E-mail: info@bookleafpub.com

ISBN: 9789357210362

First edition 2022

DEDICATION

To my village

PREFACE

Metamorphosis is curated to represent the most formative stages of my early adulthood. Through love and loss, the progression of my womanhood is beautifully captured and conveyed through this compilation. When I wrote this collection of poems, I never thought I would decide to publish them. Poetry became my avenue of expression because I was not comfortable being vulnerable with others. But, I realized that sharing my experience could help young girls, especially black girls like me.

One lesson I have learned through this journey is that in vulnerability lies freedom. When we share our innermost thoughts and feelings with one another, somehow we no longer feel alone. The enemy's desire is to shame us into a state of isolation. In that, we ultimately forfeit our healing as well as our freedom in Christ. But, we are to confess one to another as well as pray for one another as it says in the Book of James, Chapter 5. So, my prayer is that God strengthen you to break the barriers of shame and receive your healing.

Walk By Faith

Walk by faith, not by sight
Let God be your guiding light
Even though you may not see
God knows where you're supposed to be

So just let go, give God control
Trust and believe Him with your heart and soul
Don't be afraid or filled with fright
Because with God steering, you'll be alright
Why do it on your own when you don't have to?
When you're blessed to know a God who can do
all you need Him to?

So, again I say
Walk by faith and not by sight
Let God be your guiding light

Dear God

I can never fathom your mysterious ways
How you pulled that string and tucked the other to create one massive miracle
How you handled all my situations with just the snap of a finger
But I don't question you 'cause I know you're legit
People think I'm delusional but if they've ever experienced you like I have
I'm sure they'd be just as convinced
But honestly there are times where I legitimately wonder why
Like the time you allowed my friend to be snatched up with no notice
Leaving everyone in major shock
When you knew that even some would turn their back on you in their grief 'cause the pain is pure agony
And they can't imagine that God would allow this great tragedy
Honestly after that blow I don't think I'll ever be the same again
Missing someone indefinitely is a suffering I can't even explain
Just knowing there's a chance you'll never see them again

I wasn't ready to let my friend go, I wasn't prepared for her departure
Just one more good laugh
One more good time
That's all I desire
But I guess that's how everyone feels so I can't make it about me
I'll just have to wait til' I see her again…possibly

Vulnerable Heart

The depth of my love for you petrifies me
Afraid of the possibility that you may hurt me again
Afraid that I may fall so hard
That I'll become so blinded
And this will become just another cycle
A cycle of perpetual torture and excruciating pain
The pain is unexplainable yet the feeling that I get when you tell me that you love me lures me back
And I fall into your web
Hoping and praying that you're the one for me and that things will change
When in reality I'm just terrified that there's a chance that, that isn't the case
"Don't hurt me" I scream in anguish as I attempt to heal from the previous stab wound
I don't want to let you go because I'm in love with the part of you that seems so perfect
The part of you that can love me unconditionally
The part of you that can give me everything that my heart desires
And somehow I feel that the part of you that can't will just mysteriously disappear
"He can be the man I need and desire"

"People change"
"I feel he's gonna do right this time"
All things that I tell myself to cope with the fact
that I could be making the biggest mistake of my
life
Something that I don't want to admit to myself
but it's real life
I want this
I need this
I can't see myself without him
He makes me happy
Is this healthy?
Is this right?
Is this God's will?
Do I really want this?
Do I actually need this?
Is this what love is supposed to feel like?
Questions that run through my mind daily
But I never verbalize them in fear that I may
already know their answers…

Dear God: Part II

Oh God, not again
I've lost another companion, a noble friend
I cannot even process the pain
It hurts so badly, I literally can't feel it
My mind won't let me snap into reality even though every other part of me is very much aware
I can't put this feeling to words but God you know exactly what I'm feeling
It's almost like you knew this was coming so you equipped me to be steady enough for the great gush of wind that would attempt to knock me down
I don't quite understand why but I know that everything that happens is just apart of the master plan
One that no man can fathom or understand
I just know that I need you in this time
I know no other way to process this emotion unless I'm making it rhyme
Help my doubt or any unbelief
Help me to realize we just in a evil world with evil people who cause wicked things
Help me to trust you and to lean not to my own understanding

And most of all keep me from the evil things in this world and help me to make wise decisions so that I won't be the next body on a stretcher…

Everything Reminds Me of You

When I walk into a certain store, I'm reminded of us
When I hear a particular word or phrase, I'm reminded of us
There's not a day that goes by that I don't think of you at least once
At first it's cute until something snaps
And there's no longer a fondness that accompanies the thought of that person
It's aggravating because you realize how much your very existence depended upon the life of someone else
It almost feels like you've been knocked off your crutch or taken off of life support
That thing was the very reason you were even upright
And now that I write this, I realize just how unhealthy my relationship with that person was
It was my crutch, my life support, my reason for being
Then one day it was forcefully ripped from under me with no warning
There I was, left to figure it out all by myself
Figure out how I was going to make it without my aid

I had no choice but to lean on God
The pain was far too great to bear alone
And now I see that, that was the point that God was trying to make all along
You have to lean on God until it makes you uncomfortable
And that's how you know that you've began to fully trust Him

SCREAM

When you suppress all of the hurt that you've endured throughout life
You never realize how battered you actually are
Graced to live day by day unaware of your brokenness
Although your inner being screeches in anguish struggling to hold it all down
Then suddenly, minute particles of evidence rise to the surface, slowly but surely
Creeping its way up and out of the crevices that it once laid dormant
No longer hidden in the dark shadows of your heart but boldly revealing itself to you
No longer afraid to be seen
What do you do now?
Admit it
Admit the fact that you struggle to forgive yourself and others at times
Admit that you find it challenging to love when most take your love for granted
Admit that you sometimes miss those that you know aren't good for your life
Admit that you've lost two good friends to tragic deaths in four months and it hurts
Admit that you don't understand and the fact that, that in itself is daunting

Admit that sometimes fear paralyzes you
Admit that you've been stabbed in the back and you don't know who to trust
Admit that you are scared that you don't know how to guard your heart and may let the wrong people in again
Admit the lust, selfishness, and the pride
Admit the pain, admit the hurt
Admit you're broken…
You're in a broken place and that's okay
You need to be healed and that's okay
We must confess our struggles, hurts, and shortcomings to overcome them
Once you confess them, they no longer have power over you
You may be broken, but you are free
You may believe it to be contradictory
But I say, quite the contrary

Tired

When you look into my eyes what do you see?
I used to see joy and fire until life broke me
Now I see despair, suffering, and pain
Every now and then I may get a glimpse of hope
But that doesn't last too long before that is stomped on and choked
I don't want to become someone I no longer recognize
But my heart's too selfish to recognize
Frowns and sadness, that's not me
Anger and madness, that's NOT ME
Is love worth my sanity?
Is love worth the suffering of insanity?
Can't be
And if so, not to me

By You

Holding on to love because my heart won't detach itself
Causing myself unnecessary pain
Trying to love like there is no tomorrow
But instead ending up in sorrow
Because my love doesn't seem to be enough
I thought we passed this hump
I thought we were over this
But instead I find myself right back where I was wondering how the heck I got here
I wanna love and be loved
I wanna hold and be held
I wanna feel like I'm the only girl in the world
I wanna feel like a child in your arms
Clinging to your every word
And sometimes I feel like that
But other times I feel like the outcast
Just dying to grasp your attention just once, to be noticed by you... just once
Rejection after rejection
Hurt after hurt
Lesion after lesion
You'd think I would have learned my lesson
You'd think that I would get the picture
But I haven't because all I want to do is love you

All I want to do is love and be loved
Hold and be held
I wanna feel like the only girl in the world
Like a child in your arms
Clinging on to your every word
Because the only man I see is you

A Letter From The Church

Forgive us
For everything that we've said or done to make you feel less than
Not good enough
judged
Or unloved
Forgive us
For our legalism and political correctness
But also for our tendency to water down the message
Just because we think you'll receive it better
Forgive us
Our righteousness has become your condemnation
Because we sometimes forget that the same grace that we're trying to force you to accept
Is that same grace that keeps us on our feet
And the same Jesus that we are advertising to you
Is the same Jesus that we call on when we're encompassed by the illusion of defeat
We let power that doesn't even belong to us get to our heads
So we step down off of our high horse to tell you what should have been said

Like how He formed you in your mother's womb and He has a purpose for you
And the fact that nothing in, above, or below the earth can separate you from His love
And while we were yet sinners He sent His Son to die for our offenses
Or how He doesn't expect perfection but someone receptive to correction
And it's okay to be skeptical and have questions
Because doubt is the trigger that causes faith to ignite
But we can't forget that He is also just and His wrath is just as powerful as His love
And in all honesty, how we're mere mortals who make mistakes but we aim for holiness everyday
This walk ain't easy but you're not alone because God will supply his unshakable peace when you seek His face
All these years, we've gotten it wrong
Which fills us with contrition
And yes we know that the damage is done
But we hope you can find it in your hearts to Forgive us

It's Okay to Be Black

Something that we don't talk about in church often is how
Sometimes we feel forced to treat our blackness and our faith as separate entities
We get uncomfortable and we shy away from the topic because it's just too "controversial"
We feel that it will cause a divide
Well I'm sorry to break it to you church but the divide has already occurred
And it's cause is rooted in the very thing that we bury
Our blackness
See we have to realize that it's okay to talk about these topics synonymously
And that it's okay to celebrate our earthly heroes without blaspheming the Ultimate Hero who is the Savior of all mankind
And that it's okay to be black and proud as long as you don't forget who allowed himself to be humiliated for you amongst the crowd of traders
Also, that it's okay to advocate and fight for your people as long as you don't forget the one who advocated and fought for you in the Holy Courtroom

See it wasn't until I was sitting in a sociology class and was asked "what are your achieved and ascribed social status positions?"
I had to look at my golden brown melanin and womanly silhouette to see that just because Christ had saved me doesn't mean that my outer appearance disappears
I mean in his eyes we're all His children and He loves us the same no matter what your social status position may be
But in this world I was still black and a woman
And what that showed me was that God does not call us to dispose of our obvious natural identity but to place everything that we are in Him so that our inner identity portrays and glorifies Him, not us
We are to place our identity in Christ and not solely in who we are because our blackness will fade away but the God that abides within us will reign forever
So let's not forget to teach our black brothers and sisters to be proud of the melanin they possess and to understand that their hair is beautiful with kinks or tressed
While simultaneously emphasizing The One who gifted us these attributes and why it's important to tell Him yes

Hear Our Cry

Stop trying to silence the cry of my people
You can no longer cover the groans of our agony
with false narratives and flat out lies
We are treated as if we have no dignity
We are seen as the scum of the earth
Why can't anyone see our worth?
My crown sets high upon my head
And I walk with my chin toward the sky
Yet when you see me, you see dirty rags and a
hobo sack
Why?
Why do you treat me this way?
We are both flesh and blood
Skin and bones
Made up of the same anatomy
Yet, due to your ignorance, somehow I'm your
enemy
I don't mean to condescend
But are you just upset that I have such beautiful
golden melanin?
Or maybe because my hair possesses character
as it flows through the wind?
Or because my soul glows with beauty just as
my skin
Because of Christ the One who lives within?
I mean if I were you, I'd be jealous of me too

But none of that gives you any excuse
Betrayed by our own leaders and delivered into your hands
You stripped us of our names which removed a sense of identity
Generations passed no longer knowing the greatness that we possess
As you continued to degrade us until you broke our spirit
You trespassed against the rights of our humanity
Treating us as if we have no soul
God created me in his image just as you
I don't understand why it's so hard to believe that God loves me too
You WILL hear the cry of the black man and the black woman
We will no longer be ignored
How can you be angry because I want to be heard?
I've been trying to get your attention since 1776
The year is 2020 and I'm no longer asking, I'm demanding my due respect!
So until our voice is heard, we will continue to speak up and speak out
Beat me up and gun me down
My voice may waiver but I will not back down
We are bleeding from our wounds
Dying due to petty biases and hate

Your eyes have to be shut to be oblivious of the injustice that we face
But that's alright 'cause imma fight for what's right until I'm blue in the face
Imma fight until what's right don't look right no more
And even when it seems that my brothers and sisters have surrendered their gloves
Because we must push to see the day of victory that our ancestors only got to dream of

For I've Seen Love

For I've seen love and it's nothing that I've ever imagined
It's not a fairytale or a story of butterflies and fuzzy feelings
It's work, it's choice, it's perseverance
It's selflessness, dedication and openness
Sometimes you give more of yourself than you ever intended to
Love is a verb
Love is willingness and sacrifice
For I've seen love and it's a beautiful facet of experience and growth
Love builds character, love magnifies truth
Love is a noun
Love is a man
Love died for us
Love extended His hand in mercy
Love
For I've seen love
And His name is Jesus

Especially For Me: An Ode to Mom

It feels like when God made you, He made you,
especially for me
The way your words soothe me in times of
despair
The way the dip in your shoulder cradles my
head as my heart becomes overwhelmed with
reassurance
The way you support my hopes and dreams
without end
On the sidelines screaming at the top of your
lungs,
"You can do all things through Christ who
strengthens you!"
Your continuous support has propelled me
forward
And your many sacrifices have enabled me to
reach for the stars
Thank you

Forget You Always

Tears well up in my eyes as my heart races
I can no longer hide this debilitating anguish
My wounds are intangible yet the pain I feel is a physical thing
I tried to mask it with a smile but it soon began to fade away
I thought that the more time I spent with God, the more the pain would dissipate
But a wise woman once said to me, "it's always going to get worse before it gets better"
If worse was an ocean, I'd be the boat shipwrecked by the wiles of its waves
I just want to see the better days
I don't only want to hear about the sunshine on the other side
Oh how I long to finally feel the warmth of its rays upon my skin
I'm tired of crying at the sound of his name
I'm tired of the countless involuntary strolls down memory lane
I just want to forget
And at the very same time, I want to always remember
I hold on to the memory of our love because that's all I feel I have left of you
Despair tucks me in at night

But hope wakes me in the morning
I know that this is not where my story ends

For An Eternity

Needless to say, I love you
I rarely find myself speechless
But the way you make me feel confounds me
I realized a while ago that I wanted this forever
Kinda like when you're eating good and you
wish for that last bite to linger a little longer
Or like the dream you hope to never wake from
That's how I feel when you hold me
When you look me in my eyes and whisper to
me ever so sweetly
"I love you my beautiful queen"
You make me forget that I'm standing
And as Adrion said, "I never plan on landing"
You complete me
Like the last puzzle piece
And each night before I fall asleep
I pray to God that this love lasts for an eternity

The Revelation of Love

Thanks to You, I finally understand
The transcendent nature of your love
Revealed through your grace and mercy
Now shining through Christ in us

The power of Your love is unmatched
Its strength is unheard of
In the depths of Your heart toward us, its true beauty is found
Made manifest through the sacrifice of Your begotten Son

Even knowing our condition
You saw fit to save the wretch
For that, I am eternally grateful
Forever surrendering my life to You

Trust in Him

God, I trust You
I choose to forsake the comfort of my
understanding
Embracing Your infinite wisdom
God of the universe
Captain of my soul
I relinquish all control
To You

Yes and Amen

Promises of God
Free to those that are in Him
They are sure and true

www.ingramcontent.com/pod-product-compliance
Lightning Source LLC
Chambersburg PA
CBHW051752130826
49812CB00033B/1116
* 9 7 8 9 3 5 7 2 1 0 3 6 2 *